AF261520

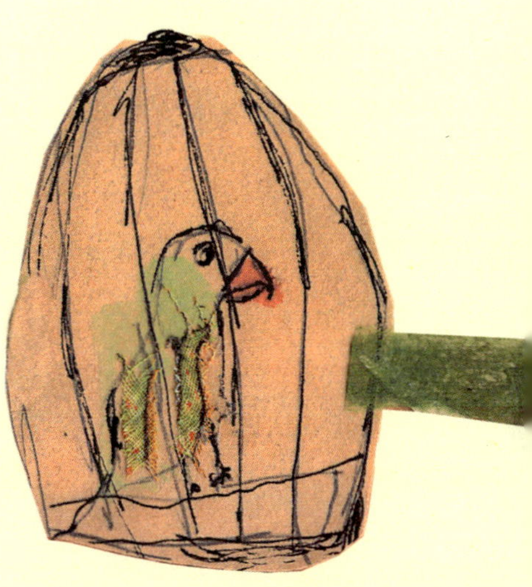

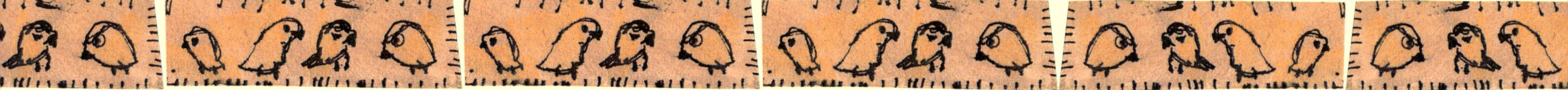

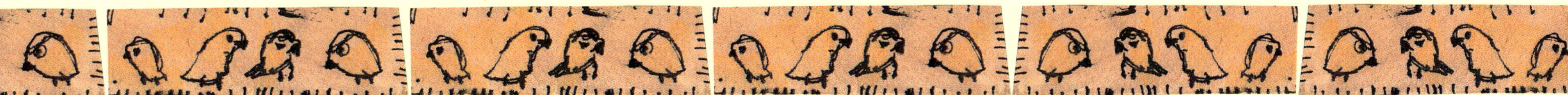

THE CROW AND THE BIRD

BAHAR TAGHIANI

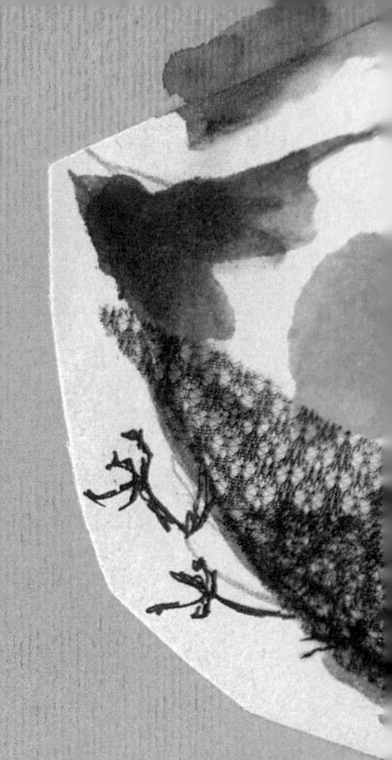

THE CROW SEES A BIRD IN A NET.

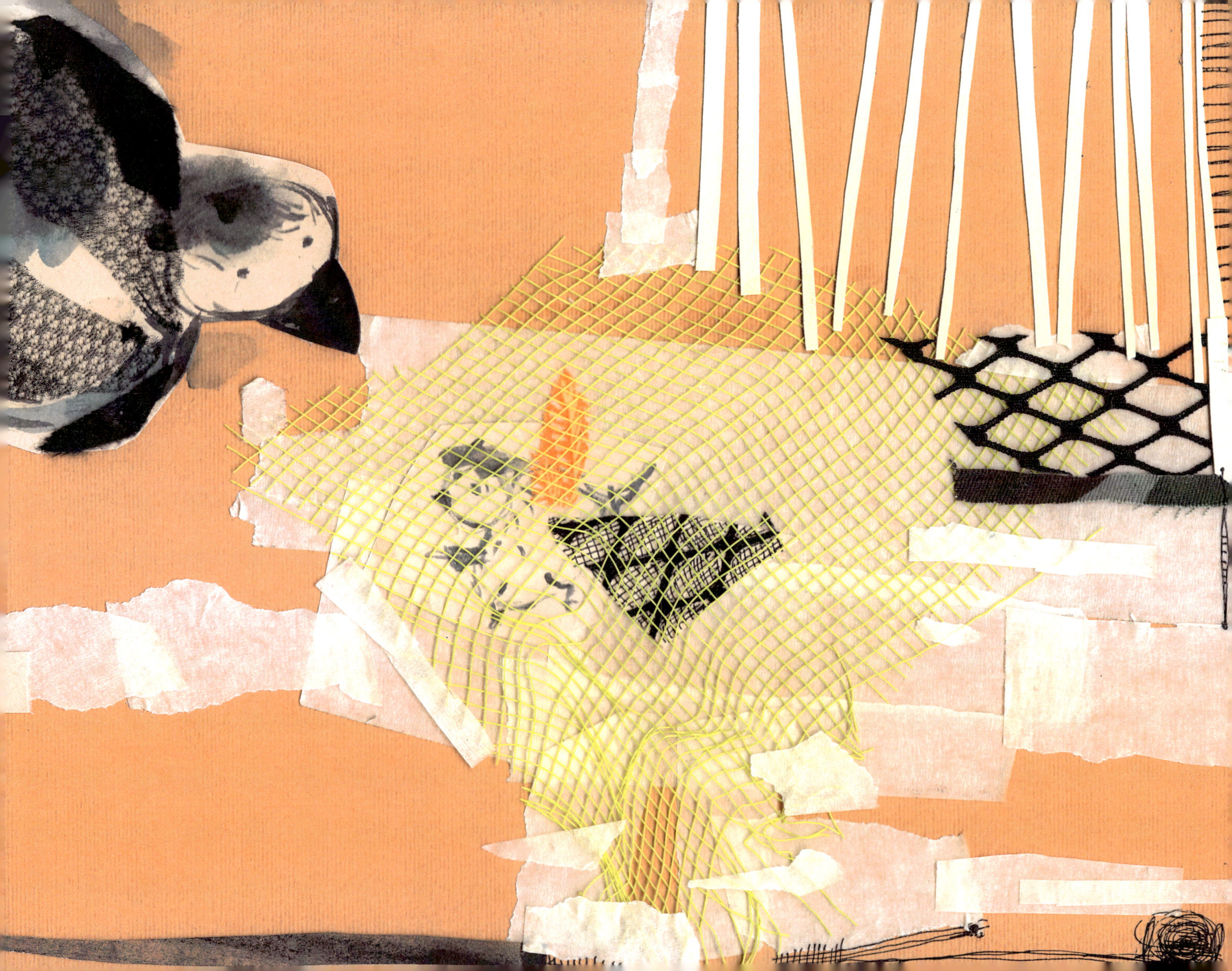

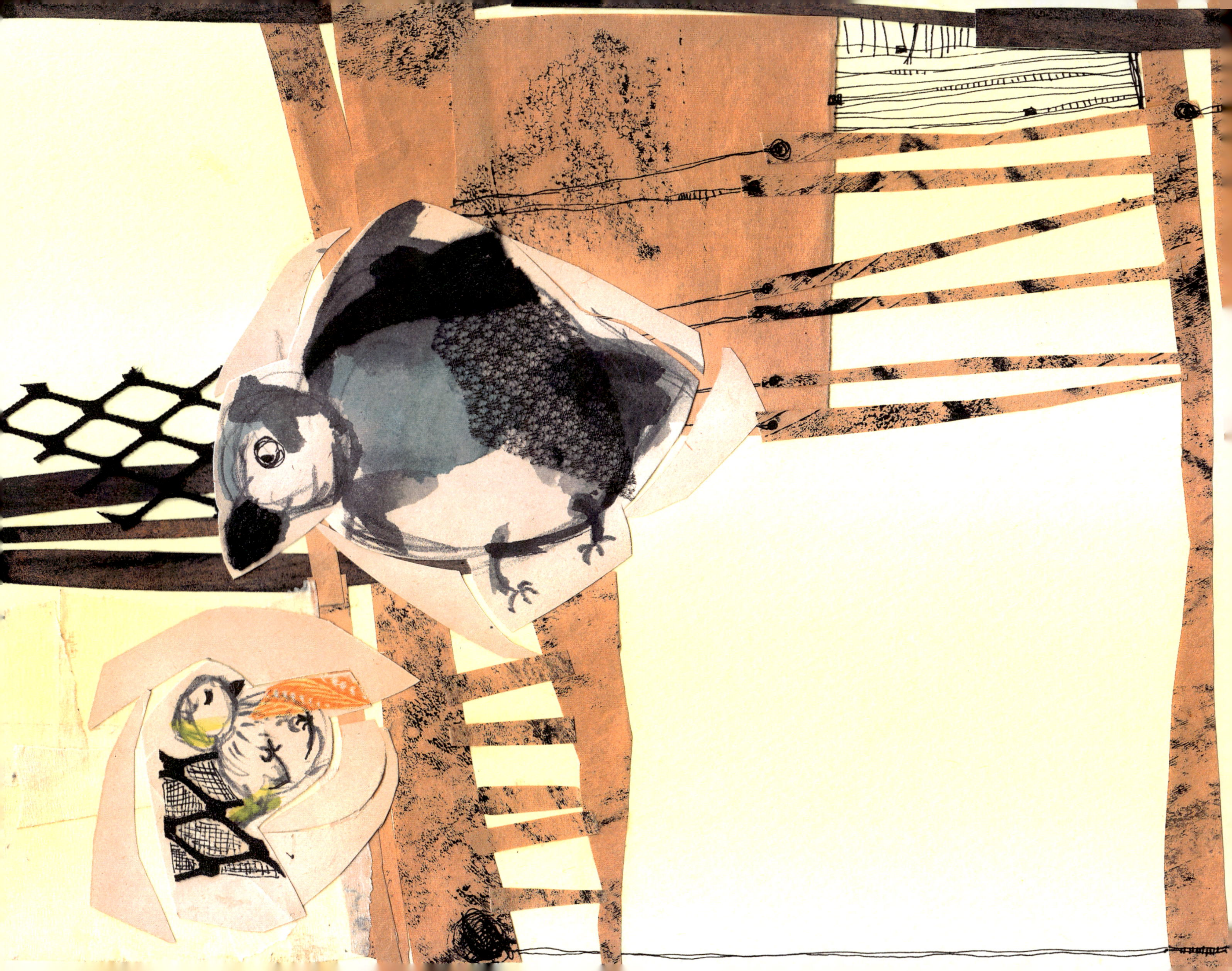

THE CROW FREES THE BIRD.

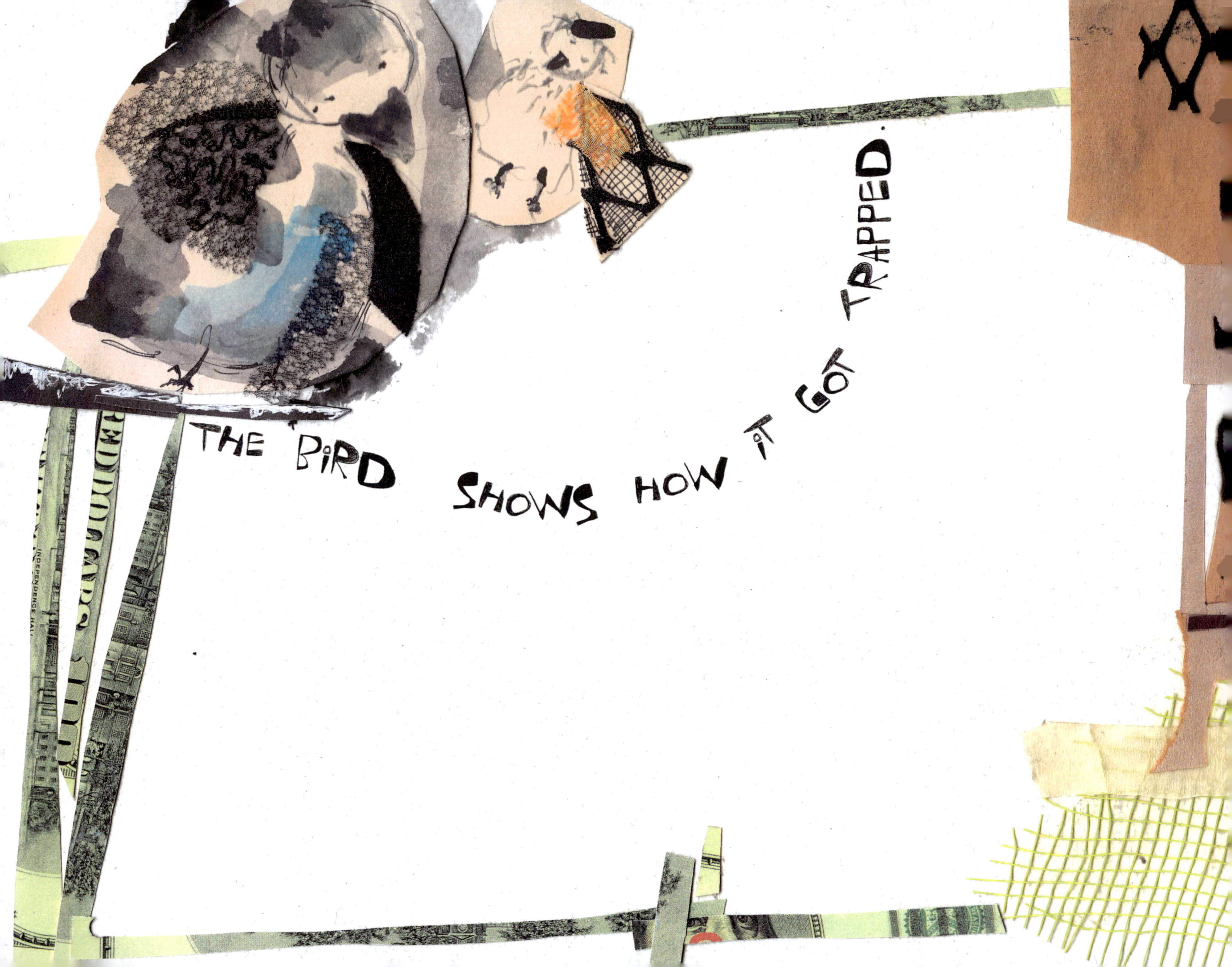

THE BIRD SHOWS HOW IT GOT TRAPPED.

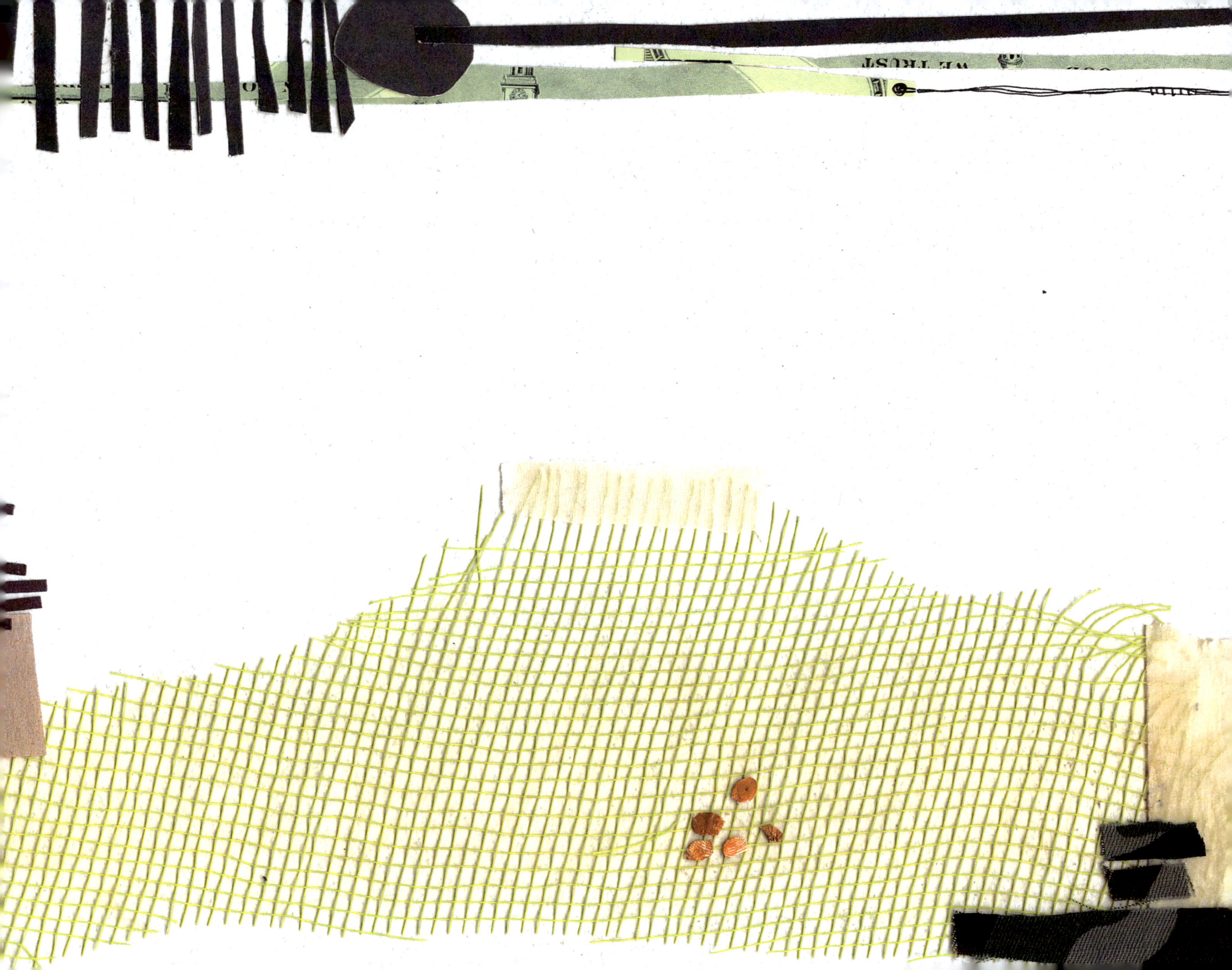

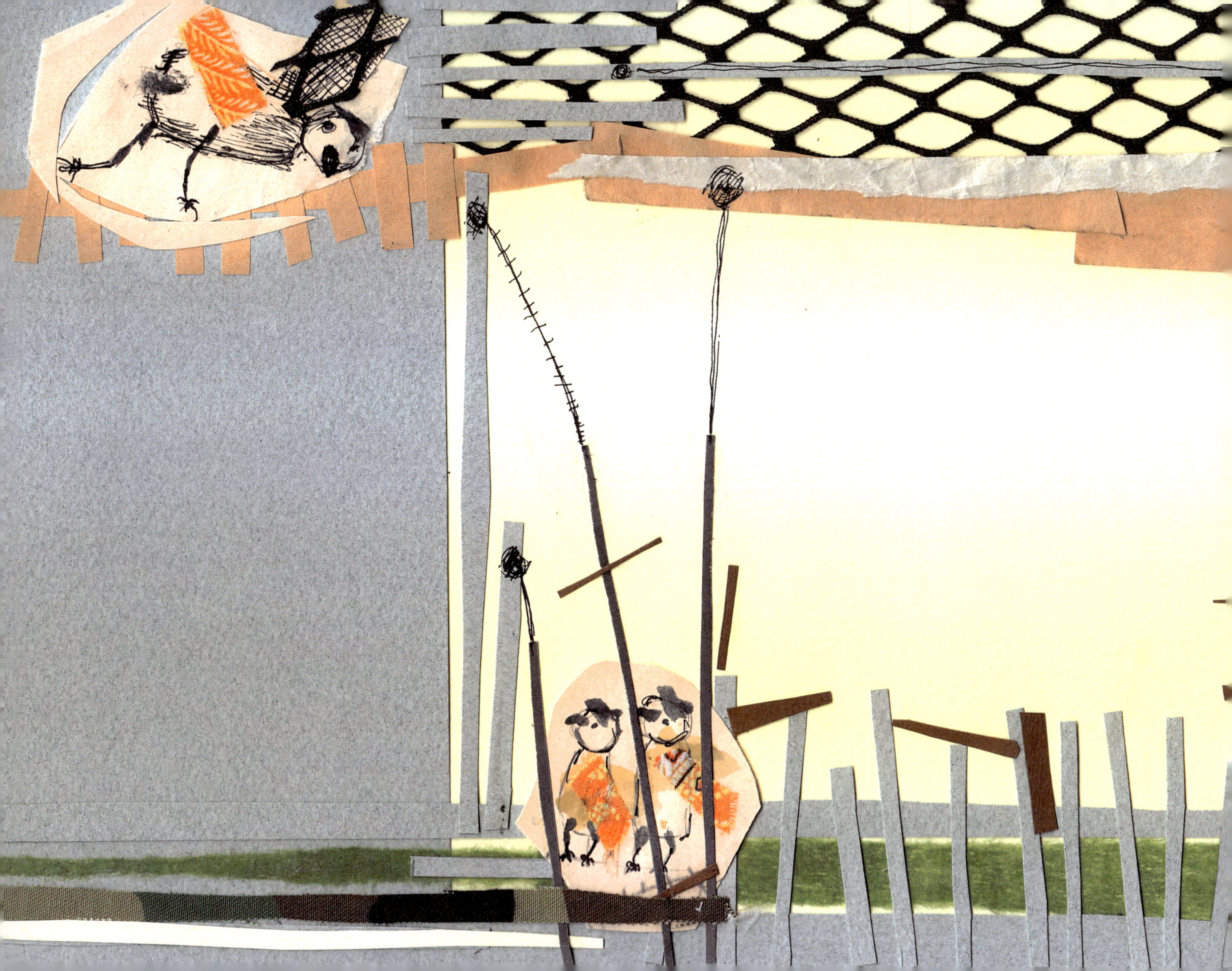

THEY FREE THE TRAPPED BIRDS.

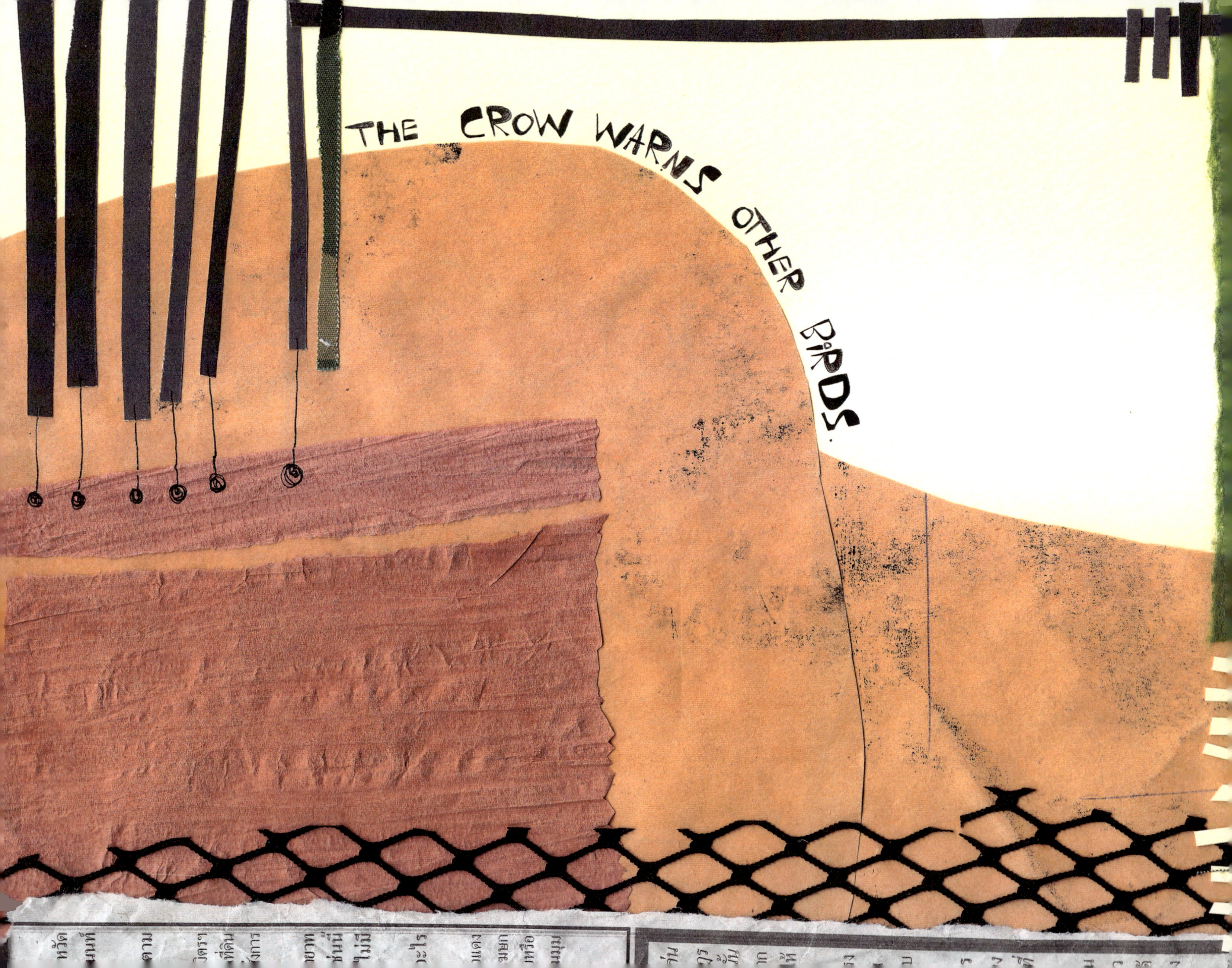
THE CROW WARNS OTHER BIRDS.

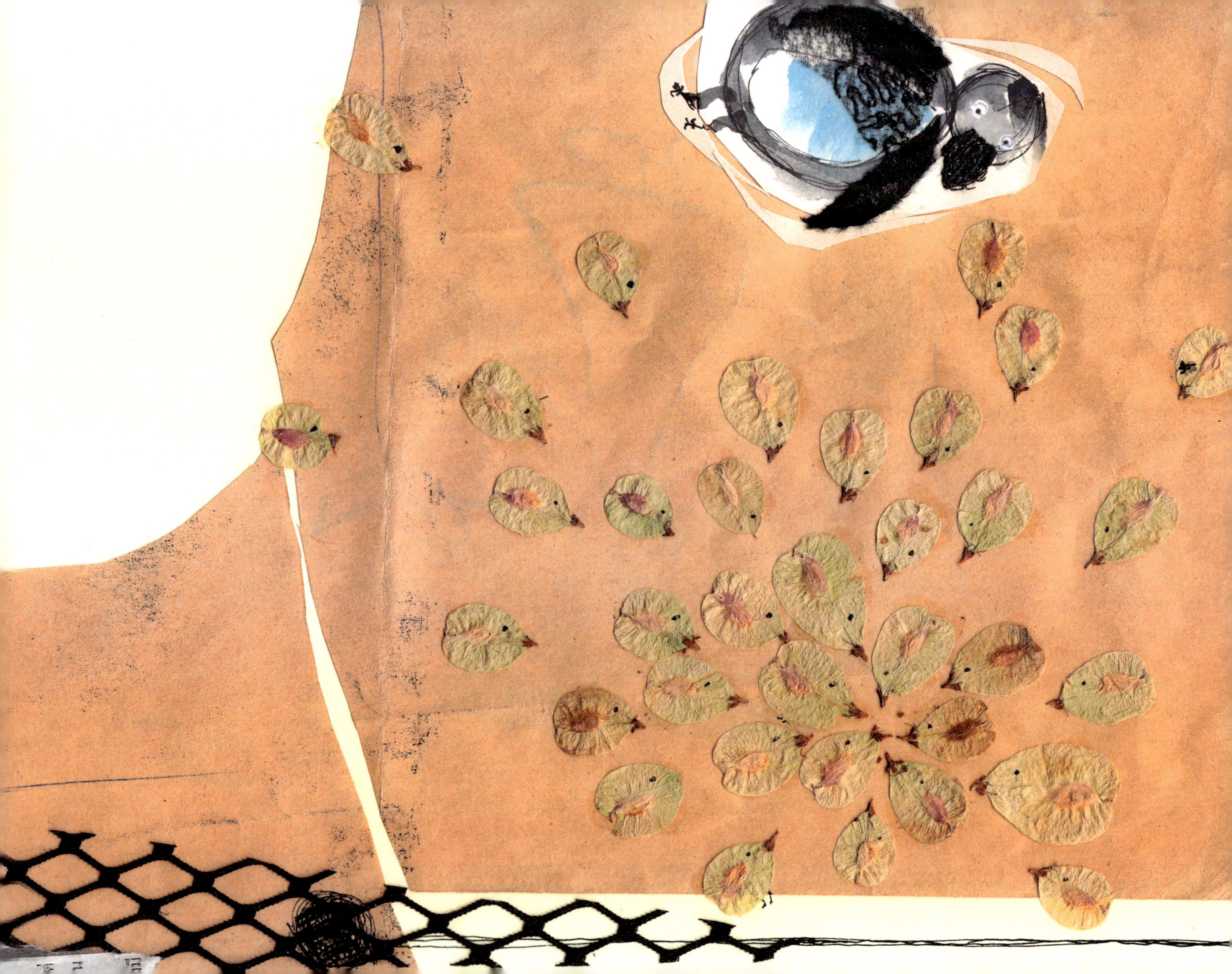

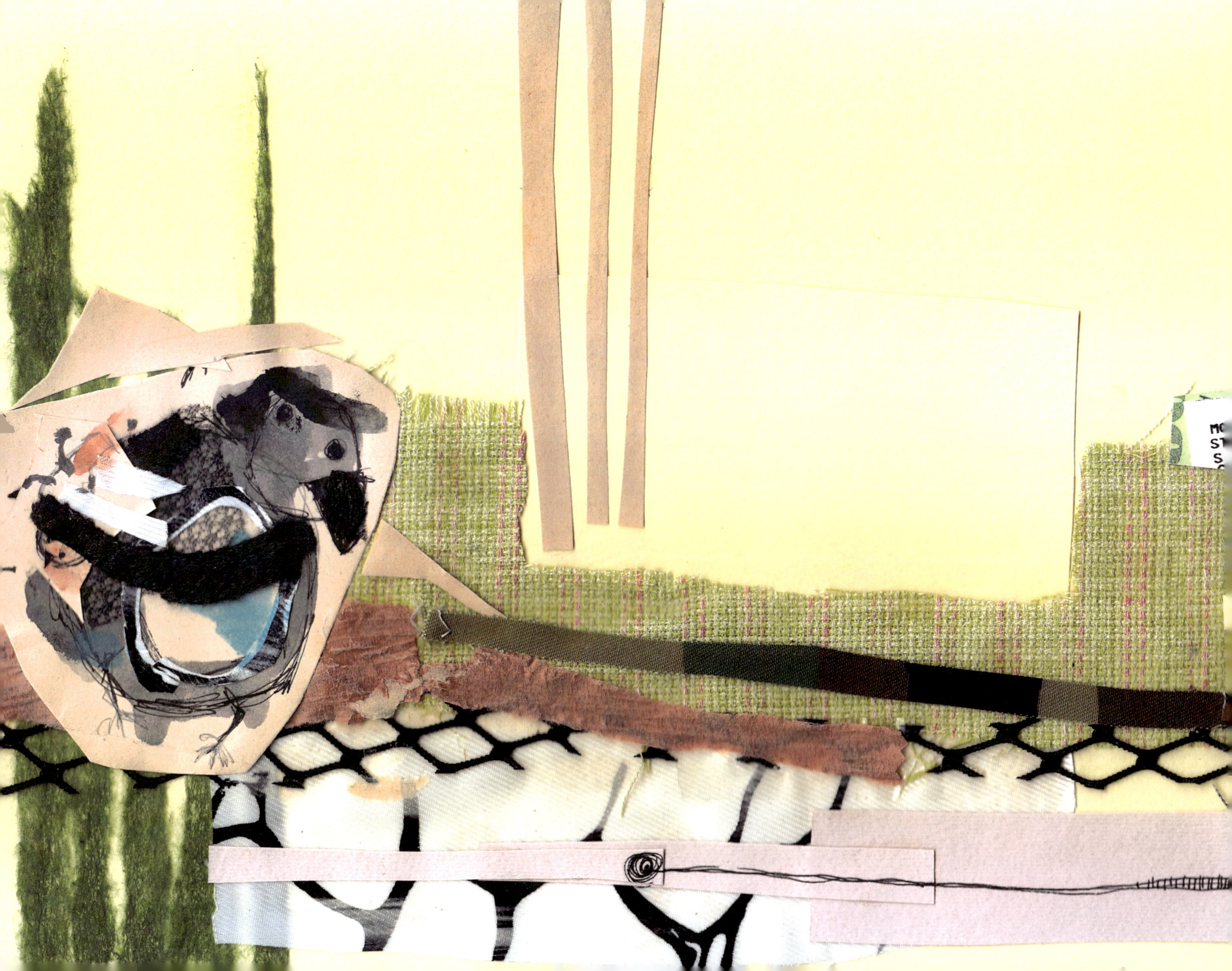
MO
ST
SC

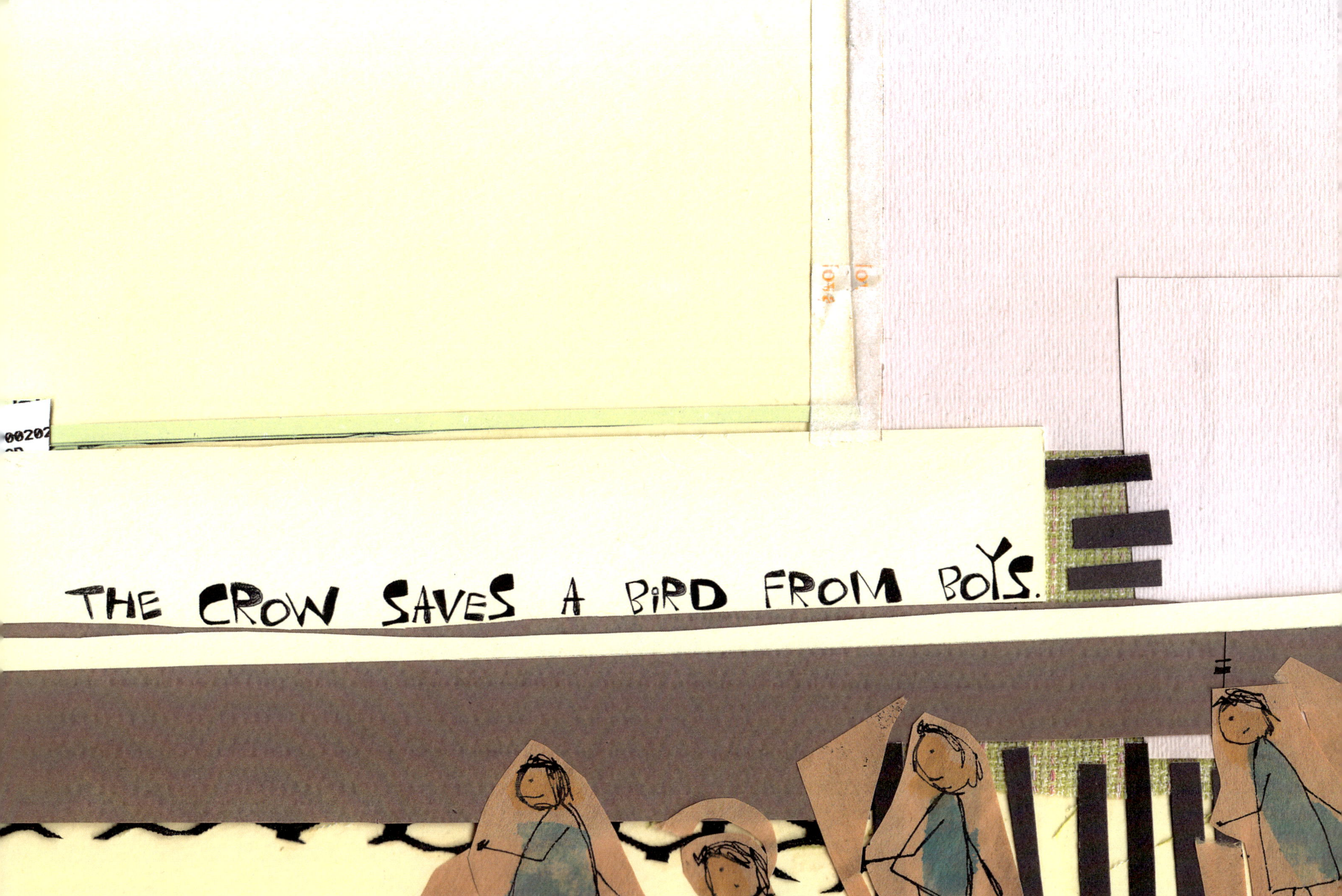

THE CROW SAVES A BIRD FROM BOYS.

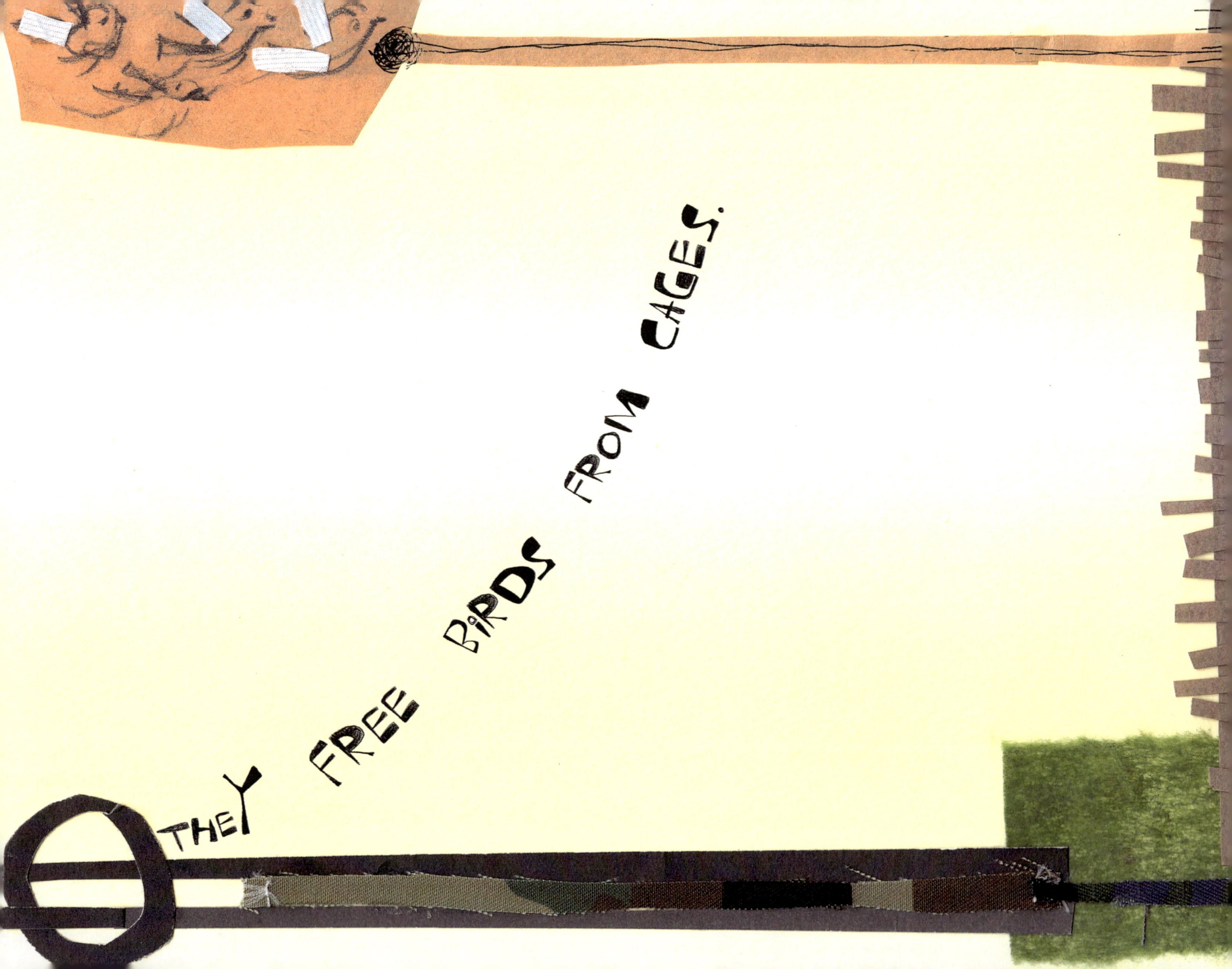
THEY FREE BIRDS FROM CAGES.

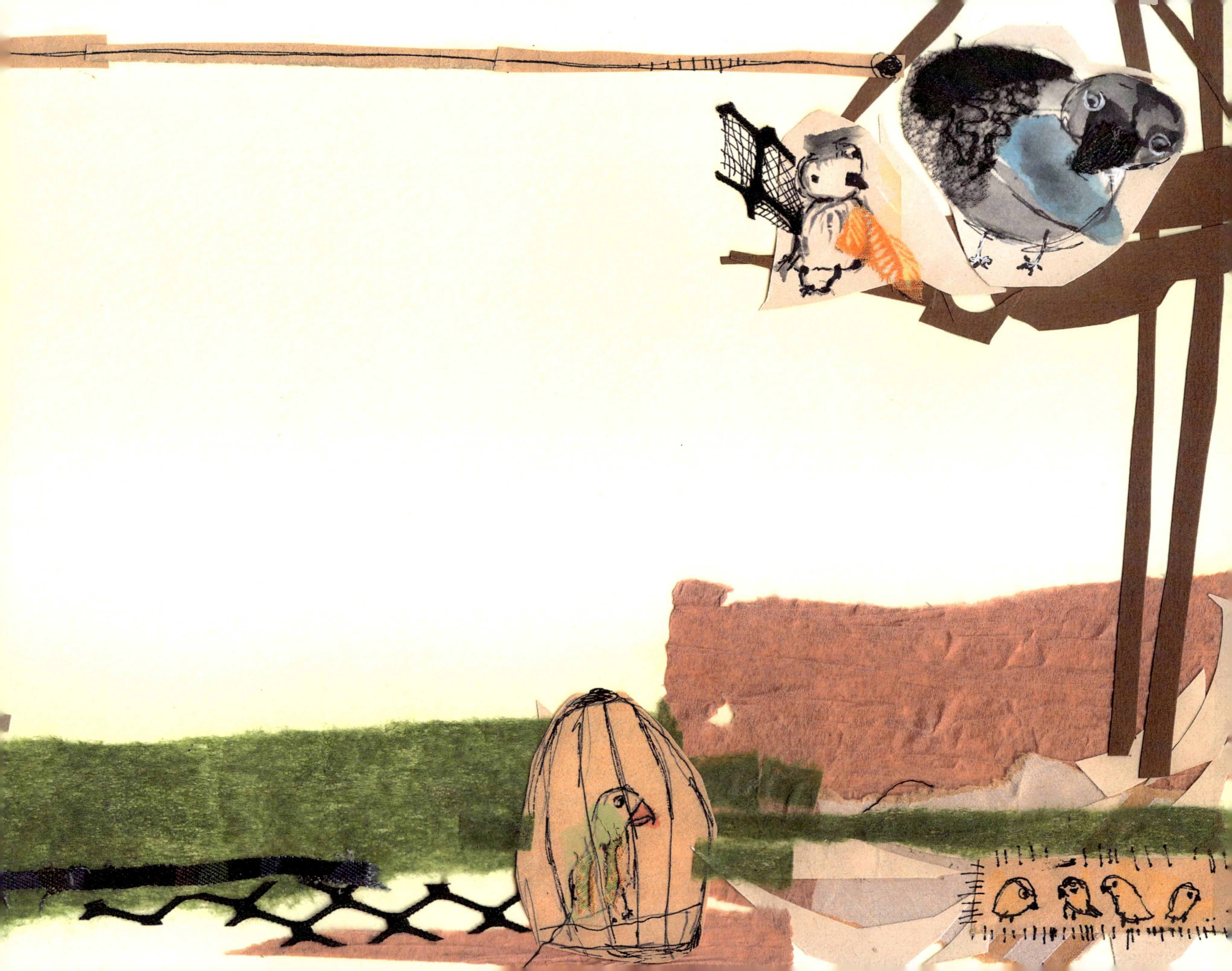

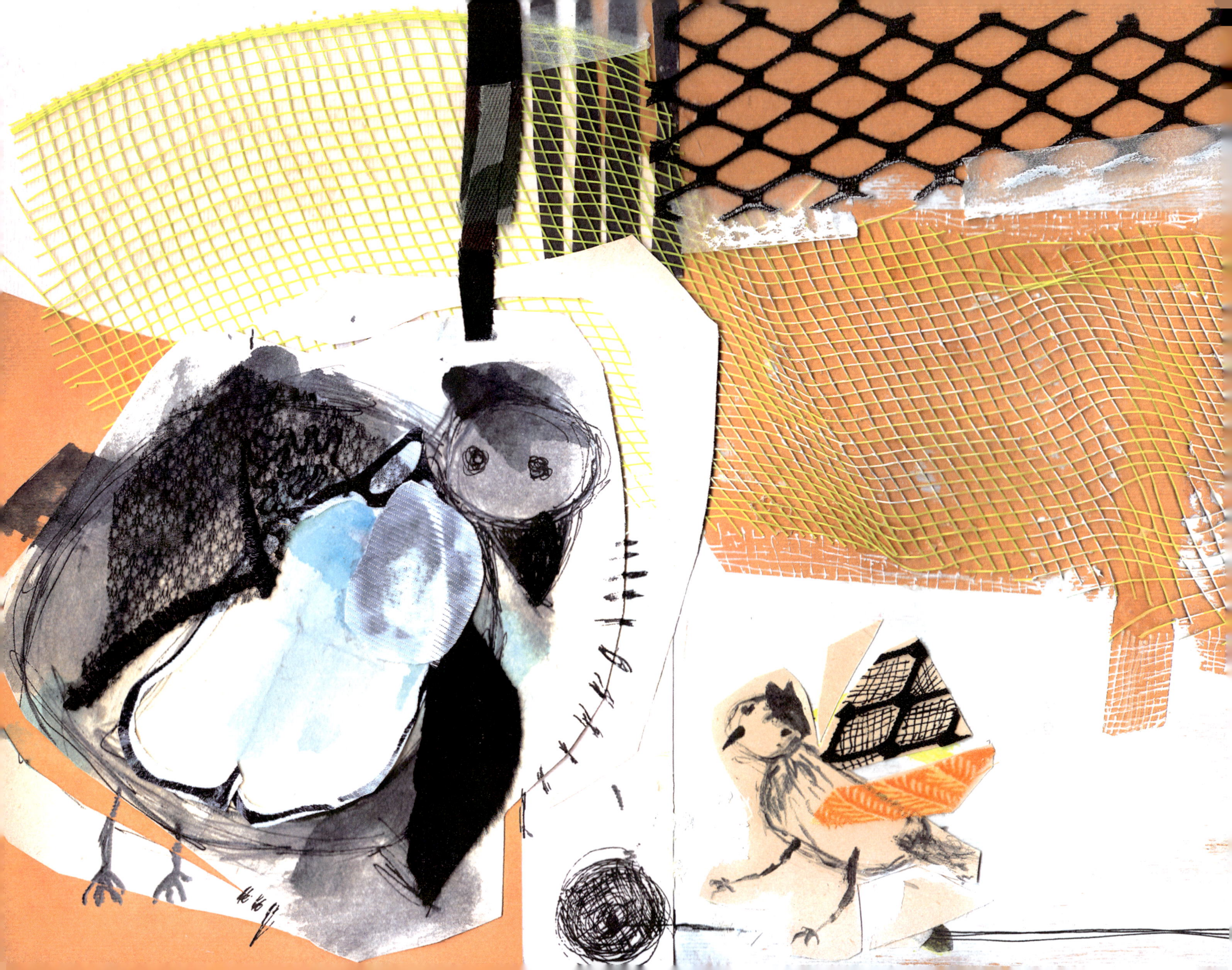

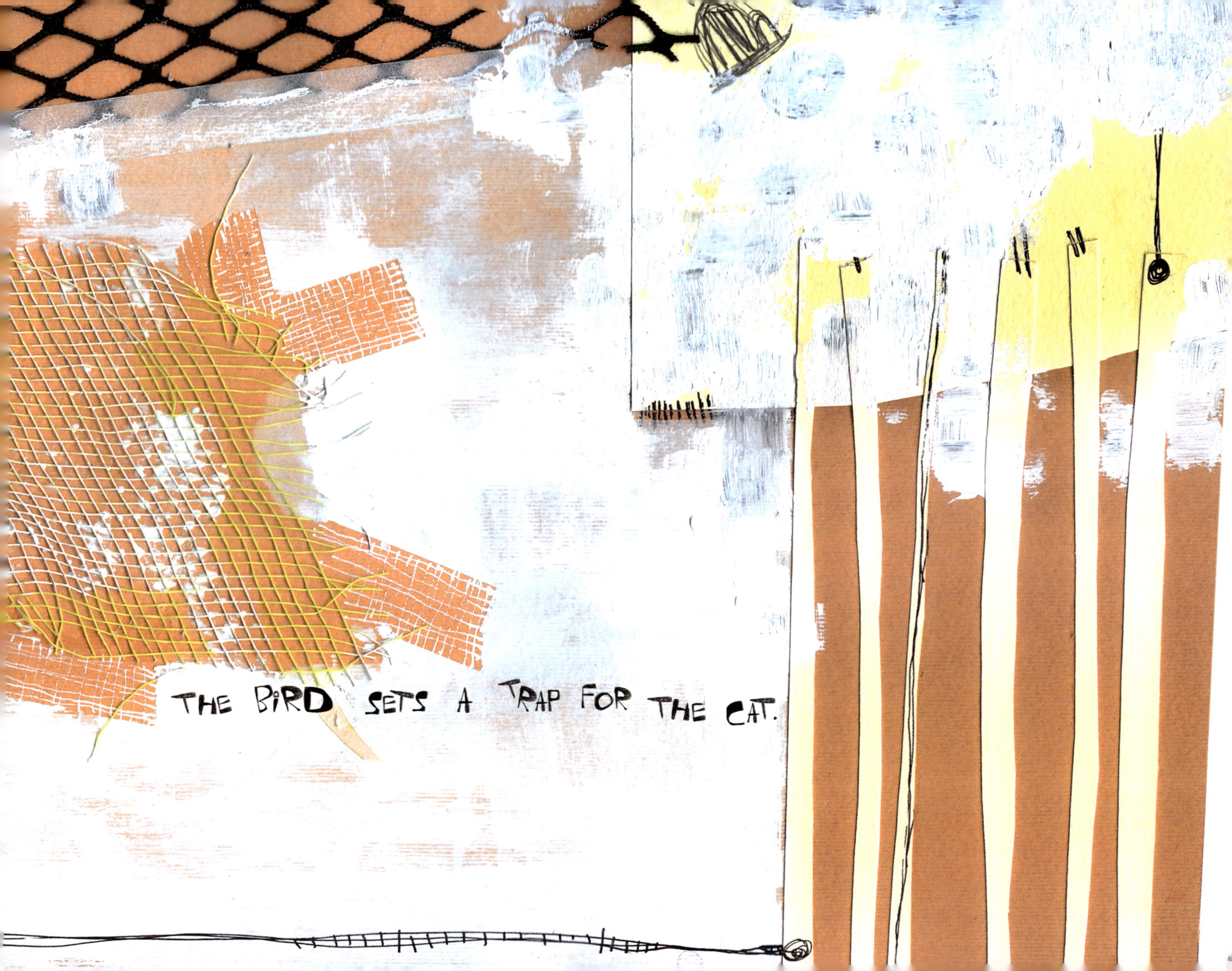

THE BIRD SETS A TRAP FOR THE CAT.

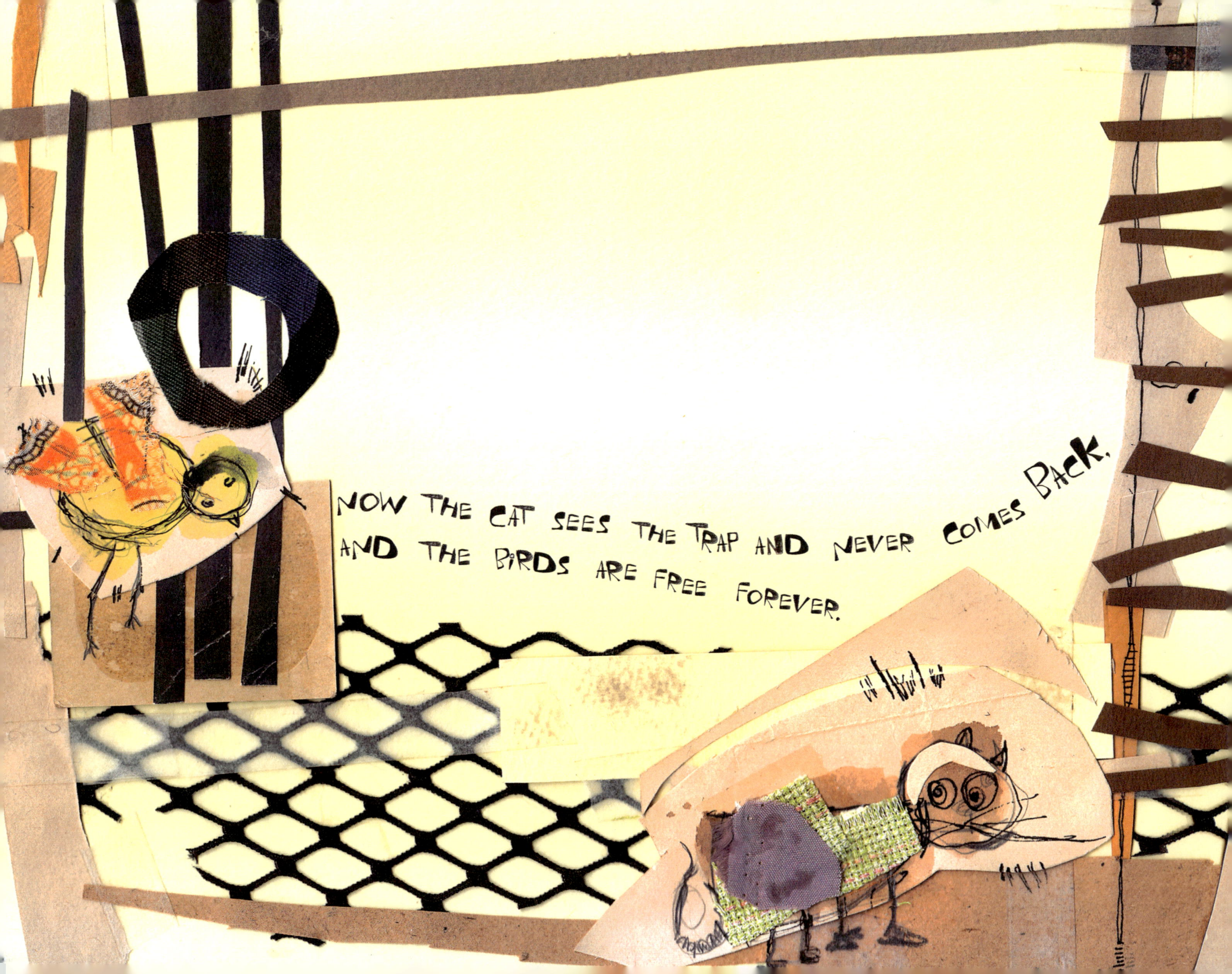

NOW THE CAT SEES THE TRAP AND NEVER COMES BACK.
AND THE BIRDS ARE FREE FOREVER.

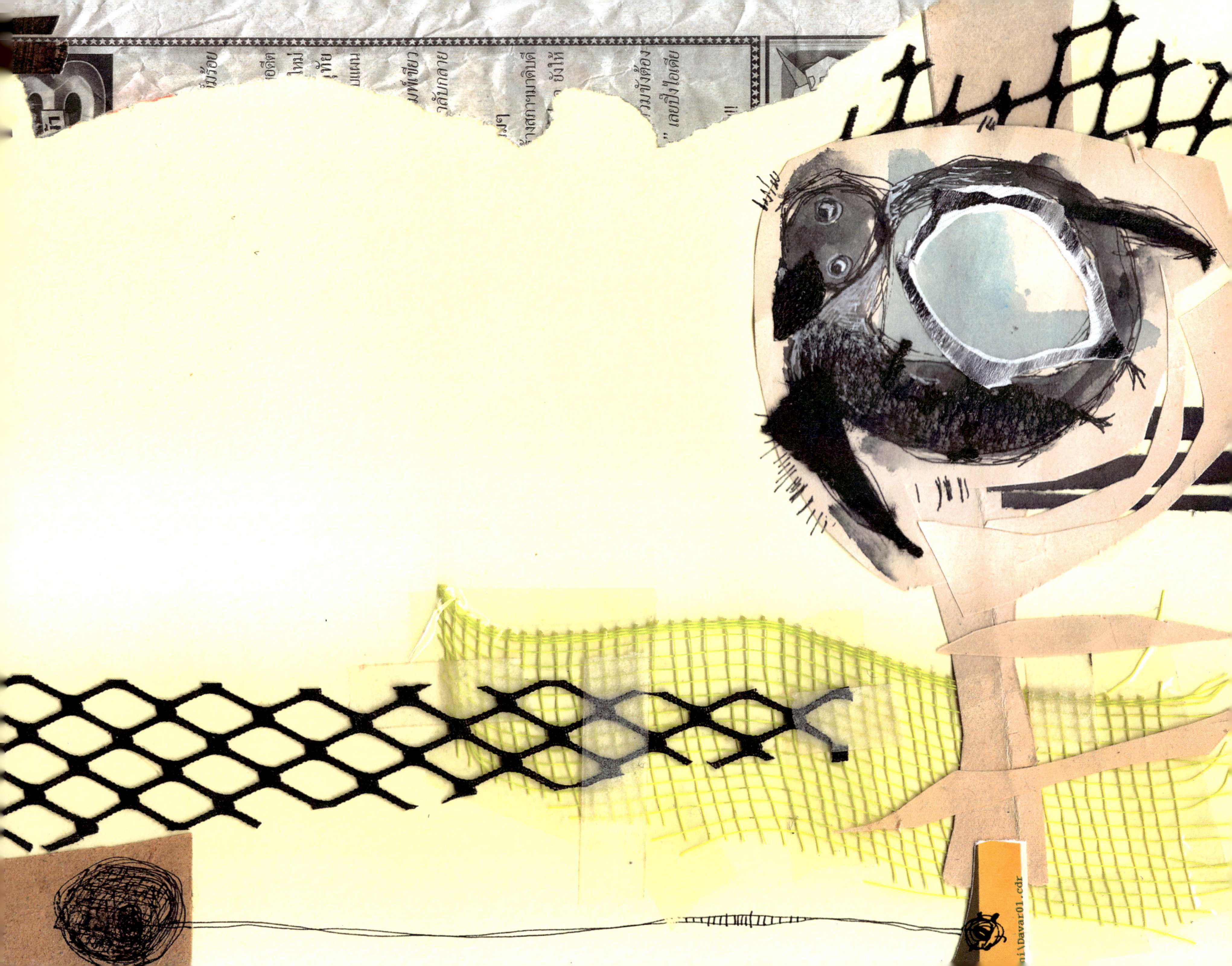
ni\Davar01.cdr

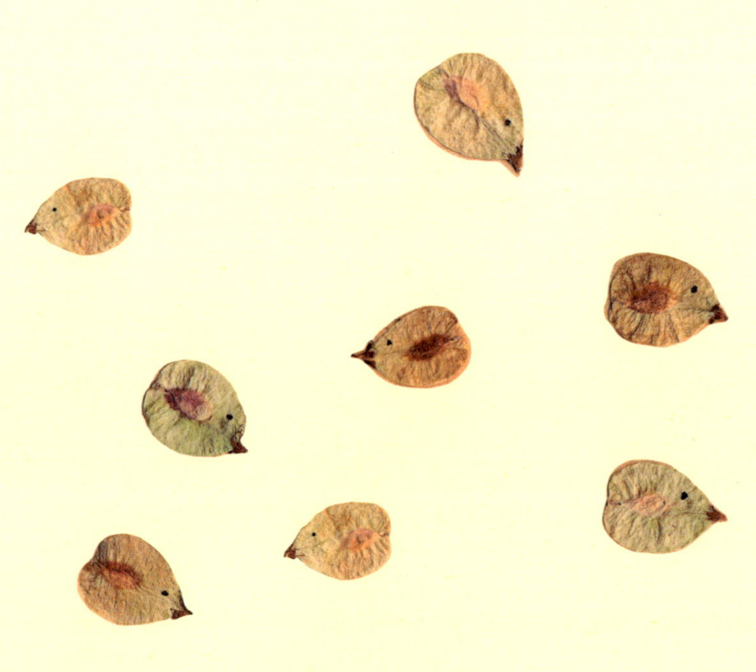

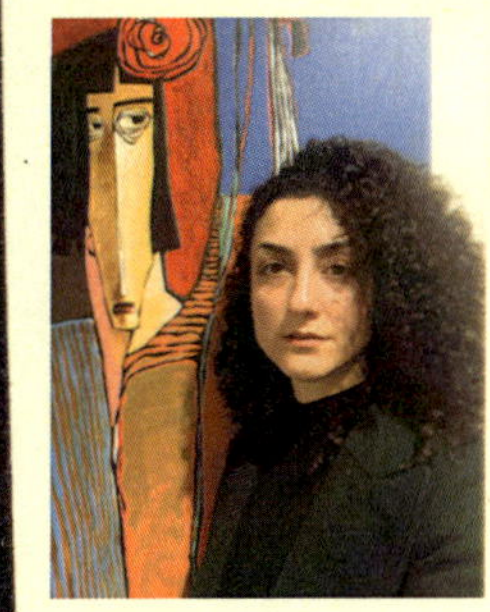

Bahar Taghiani is an illustrator and visual artist whose love for visual imagery began in early childhood. She started by creating characters out of pieces of paper, placing them in imagined stories, and bringing them to life. Today, her artworks are primarily created using mediums such as acrylic, collage, colored pencil, and watercolor, drawing inspiration from her perception of the world around her. Bahar is an award-winning artist, recognized by UNICEF for her illustration in the competition "Children on the Eve of New Year."

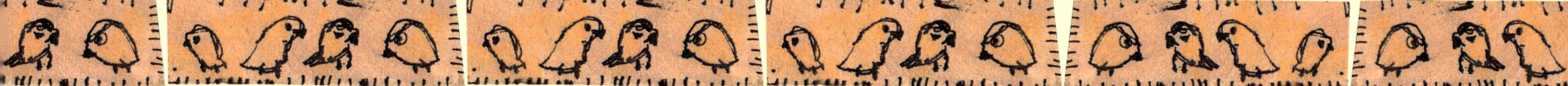

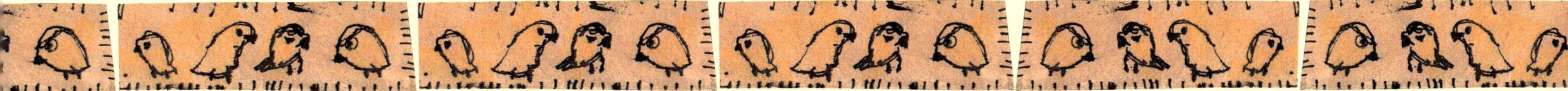

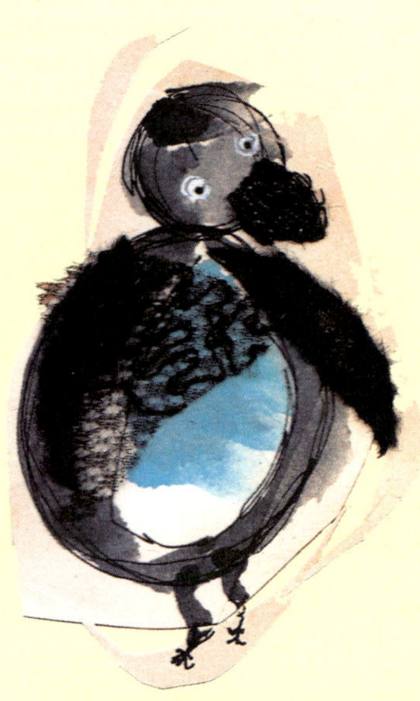

www.ingramcontent.com/pod-product-compliance
Lightning Source LLC
Chambersburg PA
CBRC101604090726
47602CB00028BA/172